Moon

my guide to the solar system

CHERRY LAKE PRESS

Published in the United States of America by Cherry Lake Publishing
Ann Arbor, Michigan
www.cherrylakepublishing.com

Reading Adviser: Beth Walker Gambro, MS, Ed., Reading Consultant, Yorkville, IL
Book Design: Jennifer Wahi
Illustrator: Jeff Bane

Photo Credits: © Onkamon/Shutterstock.com, 5; © Spacewalk/iStock.com, 7; © Aphelleon/Shutterstock.com, 9;
© Ricardo Reitmeyer/Shutterstock.com, 11; © Kevin Wells/iStock.com, 13; © Elen11/iStock.com, 15; © Serrgey75/
Shutterstock.com, 17; © Castleski/Shutterstock.com, 19; © vovan/Shutterstock.com, 21; © boxster/iStock.com,
23; Cover, 2-3, 10, 14, 22, 24, Jeff Bane

Copyright © 2022 by Cherry Lake Publishing Group
All rights reserved. No part of this book may be reproduced or utilized in
any form or by any means without written permission from the publisher.

Cherry Lake Press is an imprint of Cherry Lake Publishing Group.

Library of Congress Cataloging-in-Publication Data

Names: Devera, Czeena, author. | Bane, Jeff, 1957- illustrator.
Title: Moon / by Czeena Devera ; illustrated by Jeff Bane.
Description: Ann Arbor, Michigan : Cherry Lake Publishing, [2022] | Series:
   My guide to the solar system | Audience: Grades K-1
Identifiers: LCCN 2021036737 (print) | LCCN 2021036738 (ebook) | ISBN
   9781534199040 (hardcover) | ISBN 9781668900185 (paperback) | ISBN
   9781668905944 (ebook) | ISBN 9781668901625 (pdf)
Subjects: LCSH: Moon--Juvenile literature.
Classification: LCC QB582 .D48 2023 (print) | LCC QB582 (ebook) | DDC
   523.3--dc23
LC record available at https://lccn.loc.gov/2021036737
LC ebook record available at https://lccn.loc.gov/2021036738

Printed in the United States of America
Corporate Graphics

table of contents

Moon 4

Glossary .24

Index 24

About the author: Czeena Devera grew up in the red-hot heat of Arizona surrounded by books. Her childhood bedroom had built-in bookshelves that were always full. She now lives in Michigan with an even bigger library of books.

About the illustrator: Jeff Bane and his two business partners own a studio along the American River in Folsom, California, home of the 1849 Gold Rush. When Jeff's not sketching or illustrating for clients, he's either swimming or kayaking in the river to relax.

Moon

I'm the Moon. You see me on clear nights. Sometimes you can see me during the day!

I'm many thousands of miles away from Earth. The way I **rotate** around Earth means that you'll see only one side of me.

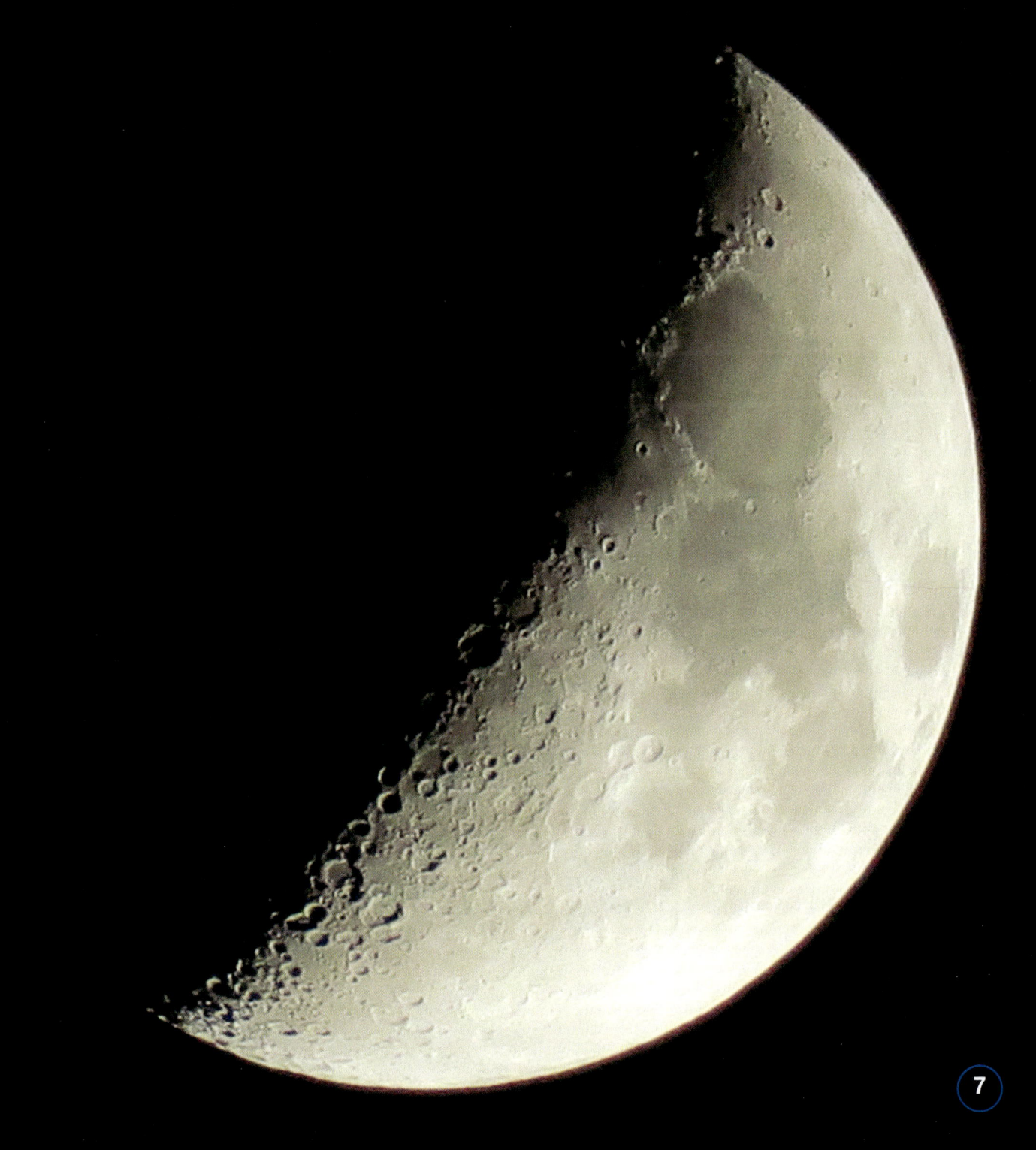

I help keep Earth from wobbling. I even help control Earth's **climate**.

6

My **gravity** controls the ocean **tides** on Earth. This is why there is high tide and low tide.

Other planets have moons. Most have more than one. More than 200 moons are in our **solar system**. I'm the fifth largest!

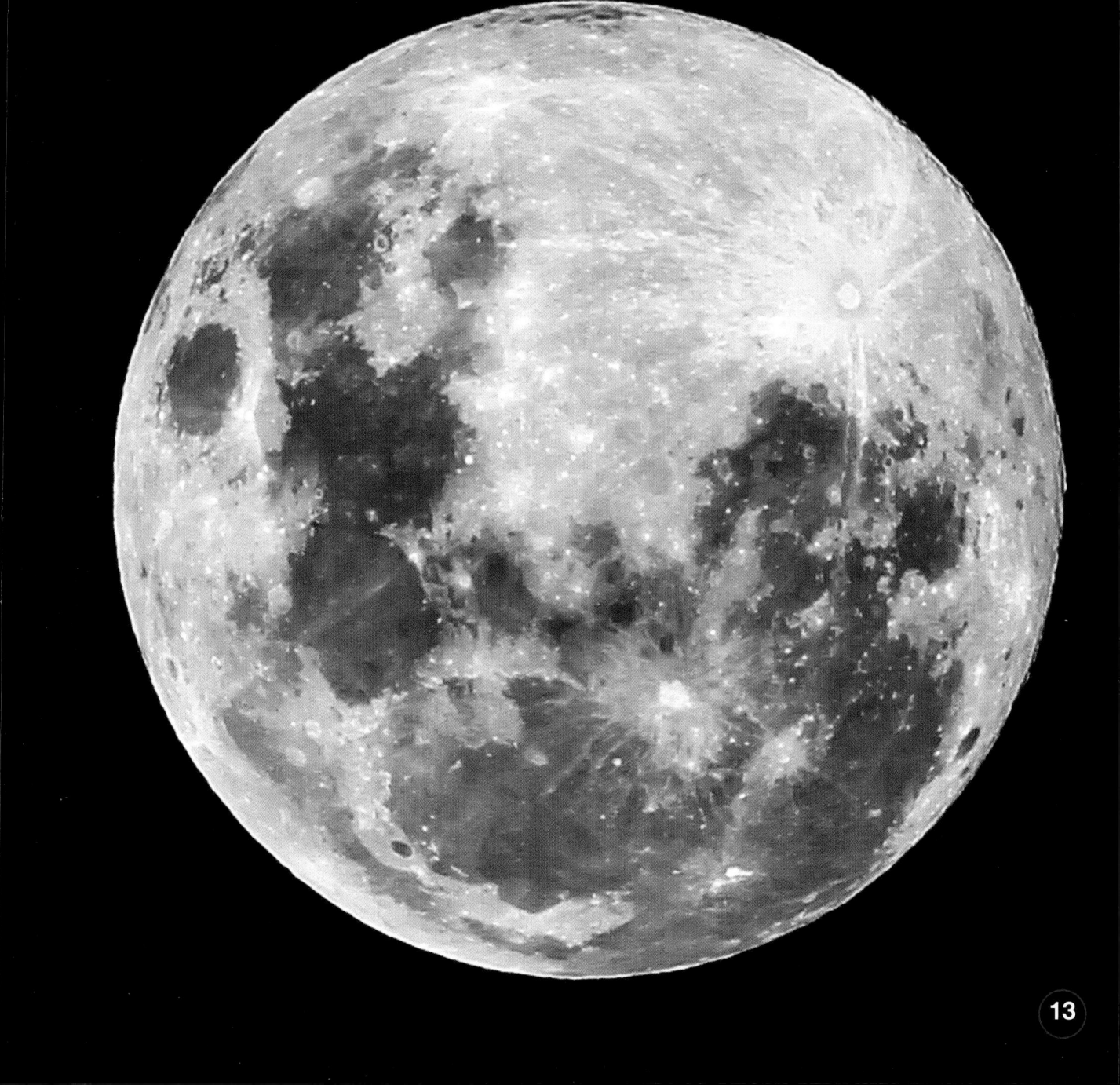

13

I have a rocky surface. It is full of **craters**. These were created when space rocks crashed into me.

15

I was most likely formed when something crashed into Earth. This object would have been really large.

My **atmosphere** is called an **exosphere**. Humans can't breathe here without a special suit.

I can't support life right now.
My atmosphere is too thin.
Also, I don't have water.

Scientists are still studying me. There's so much more to learn!

glossary & index

glossary

atmosphere (AT-MUH-sfeer) the mass of air surrounding a planet or other object in space

climate (KLYE-muht) the average weather conditions of a place over a period of years

craters (KRAY-tuhrz) holes formed by an impact

exosphere (EK-soh-sfeer) the outer region of an atmosphere

gravity (GRAH-vuh-tee) a force that attracts and pulls down objects

rotate (ROH-tayt) to move or turn in a circle

scientists (SYE-uhn-tists) people who study nature and the world we live in

solar system (SOH-luhr SIH-stuhm) a star and the planets that move around it

tides (TYDZ) the flow of ocean water as it rises and falls

index

atmosphere, 18, 20

Earth, 6, 8, 10, 16

planets, 12

craters, 14

gravity, 10

rotate, 6

solar system, 12